Dear Parent:

Buckle up! You are about to join your child on a very exciting journey. The destination? Independent reading!

Road to Reading will help you and your child get there. The program offers books at five levels, or Miles, that accompany children from their first attempts at reading to successfully reading on their own. Each Mile is paved with engaging stories and delightful artwork.

Getting Started
For children who know the alphabet and are eager to begin reading
• easy words • fun rhythms • big type • picture clues

Reading With Help
For children who recognize some words and sound out others with help
• short sentences • pattern stories • simple plotlines

Reading On Your Own
For children who are ready to read easy stories by themselves
• longer sentences • more complex plotlines • easy dialogue

First Chapter Books
For children who want to take the plunge into chapter books
• bite-size chapters • short paragraphs • full-color art

Chapter Books
For children who are comfortable reading independently
• longer chapters • occasional black-and-white illustrations

There's no need to hurry through the Miles. Road to Reading is designed without age or grade levels. Children can progress at their own speed, developing confidence and pride in their reading ability no matter what their age or grade.

So sit back and enjoy the ride—every Mile of the way!

For our cats—
Shortwick, Yo-Yo,
Phoebe and Zorro

Library of Congress Cataloging-in-Publication Data
Schade, Susan.
Cat on Ice / by Susan Schade and Jon Buller.
 p. cm. — (Road to reading. Mile 2)
Summary: Cat and Rat learn to ice skate at an indoor rink and get to be Snowballs in the show.
ISBN 0-307-26213-8 (pbk.) — ISBN 0-307-46213-7 (GB)
[1. Ice Skating—Fiction. 2. Cats—Fiction. 3. Rats—Fiction. 4. Stories in rhyme.]
I. Buller, Jon. II. Title. III. Series.
PZ8.3.S287 Cai 2001
[E]—dc21   00-034792

A GOLDEN BOOK • New York
Golden Books Publishing Company, Inc. New York, New York 10106

ISBN: 0-307-26213-8 (pbk.)   A MMI
ISBN: 0-307-46213-7 (GB)

Cat on Ice

by Susan Schade and Jon Buller

This winter will be
fun for Cat.
She has new skates.

4

And so does Rat!

The pond won't freeze.

They watch. They wait.

But then spring comes,
and it's too late!

They didn't get to
skate at all.
Next year their skates
might be too small!

"Why wait that long?"
says Mr. Deer.
"The indoor rink
has ice all year!"

The Northside Rink
is not too far.
Rat's mother drives them
in her car.

They see a poster
on the wall.

"Hooray!" says Rat.

"Let's do it now!"

"We can't," says Cat.

"We don't know how."

"How do you know?

We've never tried."

Rat pulls Cat's arm.

They go inside.

Fox signs them up.
It's not too late.
He says, "Don't worry,
you'll be great!"

"We'll teach you all
you need to know.

You can be Snowballs
in the show!"

Their Snowball suits
are round and white.

They tie their laces
nice and tight.

The trainer gives them
good advice.

Cat slips.

Rat slides.

They're on the ice!

They learn to stand,
to fall, to run.
They bump. They roll.
They all have fun.

Every day,
they come and skate.
Cat is ready.
Rat can't wait!

It's finally here!
Tonight's the night!

The rink is filled
with song and light.

The stars glide by,
so smooth and fast.

They leap and twirl.
And then, at last...

The little Snowballs
tumble in!

Cat yells to Rat,
"Look! I can spin!"

The spotlight turns
to shine on Cat.

She spins.

She stops.

She falls—KERSPLAT!

"Oh, no!" thinks Cat.
"I wrecked the show!"
But then the crowd
yells, "Go, Cat, go!"

They all love Cat.

She made them laugh.

Now they want
her autograph!